INTERNATIONAL CORP.

مع تحيّات

مؤسسة مام العالمية

With Compliments

Of

MAM INTERNATIONAL CORP.

YEMEN

John J. Nowell LRPS

Dedicated to His Excellency Ali Abdullah Saleh
President of The Republic of Yemen
and to the people of Yemen

A joint venture publication by Zodiac Publishing in association with
H & B International Agencies & Services Co. Ltd

Zodiac Publishing, Registered Office
P.O.Box 170, Churchill Buildings
Grand Turk, Turks & Caicos Islands

Zodiac Publishing, Dubai
PO Box 35121, Dubai, UAE
Tel: 09714 - 2826966 Fax: 09714 - 2826882
e-mail: zodiacpublishing@hotmail.com
www.soorah.com

Haidra & Beshari International Agencies & Services Co. Ltd.
Tel: 0967 -1 275335/275682/275685
Direct 271810 Fax: 0967- 1275513

1st published 2000
2nd print run 2001

End papers: The art of mapping developed
from ancient times and led to the compilation of future
atlases. This particular map dates from the 1850s

ISBN 0 - 9533033-2-2
British Library Cataloguing- in-Publication Data
A catalogue record for this book is available
from the British Library

Design by Nick Crawley of Zodiac Publishing
Printing by Emirates Printing Press
'A Day Above'™ is a Zodiac Publishing registered trademark

His Excellency, Ali Abdullah Saleh,
President of the Republic of Yemen

Foreword

With the approach of the tenth anniversary of
Unity Day, it is appropriate that this new book,
with a completely different perspective of our
country, should be published.

Yemen, once known as Arabia Felix - *Fortunate
Arabia* - was a unified country, until colonial
empires of the Romans, the Portuguese, the
Turks and the British sought to occupy our land.
Now, after the problems of the past centuries, we
are once again a unified nation.

Within these pages are Yemeni citizens who have
seen many changes over the past hundred years.
The older generation, more than any of us, have
witnessed the entire spectrum of change. From
the days of the Ottoman and British Empires, to
the years of the First World War, from Aden's rise
to become one of the greatest seaport in the
world to the arrival of the first aeroplanes. The
Second World War, brought an influx of allied
troops who were replaced in the mid 1960s by
advisors from the USSR. With unification, we are
now in the enviable position to seek investment
and advice from every country in the world. Our
international airports see citizens from Europe,
North America, the Far East and South Africa. All
are welcome.

This book provides a timely reminder that our
country is one of the most beautiful and historic
countries in the world. Yemen has inspired
visitors for centuries with its diversity, from the
coastal plains by the Red Sea, to the eastern
jebels stretching from Mukallah to Hawf, from
the hidden valleys in the interior, with their own
superb architecture, to the barren desert of the
Rub Al Khali and the green beauty of the
mountain.

After our recent turbulent past, no one can doubt
that the immediate future will be difficult in
many ways. We should all remember that we live
in a country with untapped resources and
stunning beauty. We now have the framework to
live and work together, both Yemeni Nationals
and expatriates of all nationalities. We should all
work together to develop our country and to
welcome the many tourists who are curious about
our historic and beautiful land.

His Excellency Abdul Malik Mansour
Minister of Culture & Tourism

Contents

This page: An inbound dhow passes, like ships in the night,
an outbound fishing vessel

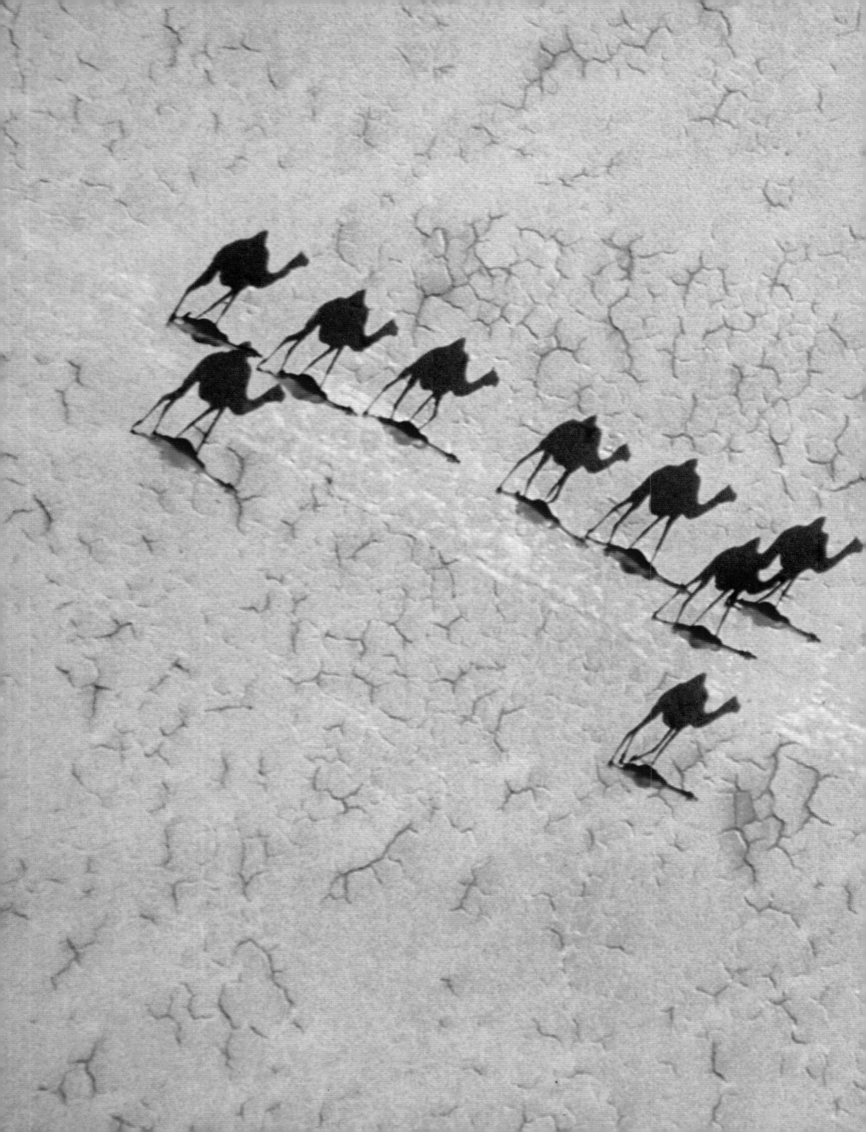

Introduction

Yemen is, and always has been, the pivotal point of the Arabian Peninsula. With the drifting apart of ancient Gondwanaland, the ancient rocks of the Arabian Plate both pulled and pushed forming the Great Rift Valley to the east and south, the Zagros and Hajar Mountains to the north. The movement still continues with the Red Sea widening at a rate of 1in (2.4cm) every year. Recent finds of dinosaur bones suggest that the region was once much wetter than it is today. Tropical forests spread across the land forming the oil-bearing strata that present civilisations depend on today.

The ice ages saw the sea levels varying dramatically. During these periods a narrow straight, just 20 miles (32 kms) wide, called the Bab Al Mandab formed a land bridge and dam wall to the Red Sea. While this land bridge was in existence, ancient breeds of animals crossed to other continents. Our own ancestors, homo erectus, are thought to have migrated northwards along the rift valley to cross the land bridge. Recent finds in the African section of the Rift Valley date the likely emergence of homo sapiens to some 200,000 years ago. The migrants put down roots, in the Nile, Euphrates and Indus valleys. They formed some of the greatest civilisations that the world has ever known.

Prehistoric settlements have been found in various parts of Yemen. Archaeologists recently discovered that irrigation in the Marib Oasis dates back five thousand years. The ancient kingdoms developed around large wadis between the mountains and the great desert. The kingdom of Saba, with its capital at Marib, was the most powerful. The great Marib Dam, built to harness and exploit the seasonal floods by means of an elaborate irrigation system, provided sustenance for some 30,000 inhabitants and was counted among the wonders of the ancient world. The Sabaeans were not only great builders and technicians, but also successful traders.

The most famous resident of ancient Yemen was the Queen of Sheba, whose unimaginable wealth and prosperity was due to the frankincense trade. She is said to have visited King Solomon during the 10th century B.C. taking with her an abundance of gold and spices. Challenging Solomon with riddles, she eventually capitulated to his wisdom and accepted his God. This exotic story has sparked the imagination of countless generations and has found entry into three Holy Books: the Bible, the Ethiopian Kebra Nagast and the Holy Koran. Although little is known about this legendary beauty, her magnificent image can be found depicted in many art forms in Yemen. There are many myths and tales associated with

the Queen of Sheba, but the majority of them seem to have little truth as barely any facts are known about her and her life in these times.

Yemen meaning "in the south"got its name from its geographical location on the Arabian peninsula. The Greeks and Romans called the southern part of the peninsula "Arabia Felix" (Fortunate Arabia), glorified by the fabulous wealth and the richness of its agriculture. The extremely fertile soil found in this southern extremity produced an incredible frankincense harvest, which was much in demand in the lands around the mediterranean, leading to the development of the frankincense trade route. The long, arduous journeys would have never been possible without strong, sturdy beasts to carry the immense loads. It is widely believed that the camel was domesticated (around 1500 BC) for this purpose. Long caravans bore this precious cargo to Petra and Ghaza and then on to distant lands. Incense was an item of high prestige, burnt in large quantities in the temples of the Mediterranean. Frankincense has always grown naturally in lower Hadhramawt and the Dhofar region of Oman. Among the other luxury goods supplied by Sabaean merchants were spices, ebony, fine textiles from India, rare woods, animal skins and gold from East Africa. In order to secure their trade monopoly, the Sabaeans kept the origin of their merchandise a secret. Once the Yemenis discovered that they could harness the monsoon winds to sail north along the Red Sea, the long land route became obsolete. They could not only reach their destination faster; they could transport greater amounts of cargo than the camels could carry.

At the end of the second century A.D., a new power emerged in southern Arabia: the Himyarites, who eventually conquered Saba and established rule over all Yemen. They brought great changes which eventually led to the decline of social and religious structures. Negligence caused the final destruction of the Marib Dam in 570 AD., causing thousands of Yemenis to emigrate to the north and east. New countries now known as Oman, The United Arab Emirates, Qatar and Bahrain grew from these enforced migrations.

Judaism and Christianity spread among the people, and the old celestial gods lost their power. Eventually, Yemen became deeply involved in the Persian-Byzantine power struggle. In 530 A.D. a joint Himyarite and Persian army co-operated to free Yemen from Ethiopian colonists. The Persians remained in power until the arrival of Islam in 628 A.D. The emergence of Islam sparked a

spiritual revival in the region, profoundly changing and reshaping the Middle East. From the earliest years Yemenis had sought out the Prophet and had joined his cause. Islam has done more to form Yemen than any other religion or ideology. In the Islamic conquest of 7th and 8th centuries, Yemenis constituted a large part of the Islamic forces. Settling down as far away as Tunisia and Andalusia, they excelled as architects, administrators and merchants. Yemen became a province at the southern edge of the large Islamic Empire. Due to its remote geographical locations, a number of small states and semi-independent kingdoms were established in rapid succession, controlling various parts, and sometimes all of Yemen from different capitals. Among these was the Zaydia Kingdom (821-1012), where the first University of Islamic learning and Natural Science in South Arabia was established. It is said algebra was invented here. Another important centre of Islamic learning is the Great Mosque of Sana'a, which still boasts an extensive library of hand-written books. The Souleyheia dynasty ruled much of Yemen from 1046 to 1138. Queen Arwa bint Ahmed (the second Queen of Sheba), ruled the whole of Yemen from her small town in Jiblah for over 60 years until her death at the age of 92. Ta'izz became the capital in 1174 under Turan Shah al-Ayyubi, the brother of the famous Salah Addin. It was the centre of a splendid Sultanate, under the Rasulid dynasty from 1229 -1454, a period of great wealth and building activity. The Zaydi dynasty of Saada lasted longest and was overthrown in 1962.

With the discovery of the sea route around Africa to India, Yemen quickly gained strategic importance to European powers with first the Portuguese and then the British taking an interest. The interests of the Europeans frequently clashed with rulers in Egypt and the emerging superpower of the Middle East, the Ottoman Turks. The Turks occupied Yemen in 1538, but fierce resistance led to their expulsion in 1635. During the 16th and 17th centuries, Yemen experienced another prosperous period when the world discovered a new drink originating from Yemen: Coffee. Holding the world production and trade monopoly of the coffee bean, Yemen allowed British, Dutch, French, and later American trade missions and factories to be established at the Red Sea port of Mohka. Coffee production declined steeply after the European powers established plantations in their own colonies in other parts of the world. Attempting to secure the trade route to India, the British occupied the port of Aden in 1839. This prompted the Turks to safeguard their interests along the Red Sea by taking the northern part of Yemen in 1848. The border between North and South Yemen was fixed by the two colonial powers in 1905.

After the Turkish withdrawal in 1918, North Yemen became a sovereign monarchy, ruled by the Zaydi Imam Yahya Hameed Addin. The Imam was assassinated in 1948 but within a week, his son Ahmed regained power over the country assisted by the northern tribes. Reigning from Ta'izz, he followed his father's outdated, style of government. When Imam Ahmed died in 1962, his son Al-Badr took power. Al-Badr supported revolutionary forces during his father's regime, but when he gained power he turned against the revolutionary forces and vowed that he would follow his father's line. On 26th September 1962, these forces led by Colonel Abdullah Al-Salal proclaimed the Yemen Arab Republic with Al-Salal its first President. Imam Al-Bader had escaped to the north and started a civil war with help of the tribes loyal to him. The struggle of Yemenis to defend the republican system lasted until victory was achieved after the Seventy Days siege of Sana'a city in 1968.

Aden received the status of a British Crown Colony in 1937, while the rest of South Yemeni territory became the "Aden Protectorate " upon conclusion of peace treaties with 1300 tribal chiefs. The "Federation of South Arabia" sought to give the protectorate a new political and administrative structure. However, the South Yemenis wanted to establish their own sovereign state. Two competing liberation movements started armed resistance in the late 1960s. Britain withdrew her forces in late 1967 leaving power in the hands of the NLF. A Soviet-style "People's Democratic Republican of Yemen (PDRY)", South Yemen was the only declared communist state in the Arab world.

Unification had always been the declared goal of the two republics but ideological differences and conflicting interests seemed to make a union impossible. A treaty was signed in October 1972 between the two governments to negotiate the terms of unification. The declaration was renewed in 1979 though another border war erupted. On 30 November 1989, a draft constitution for the unified state was signed that envisioned a mixed economy, a political system of parliamentary democracy, Islam as the official religion and Sana'a as the historic and political capital. Unification was declared in Aden on 22nd May 1990. Freedom of the press and a democratic, multi party system was introduced. After a transition period of 36 months, the first all Yemen parliamentary elections were held on 27 April 1993. Administration and economic reforms were progressively introduced which further benefited the unity of Yemen. Subsequent elections were held in 1997 and direct presidential elections were later held. Yemen celebrated the 10th anniversary of Unity Day on 22nd May 2000.

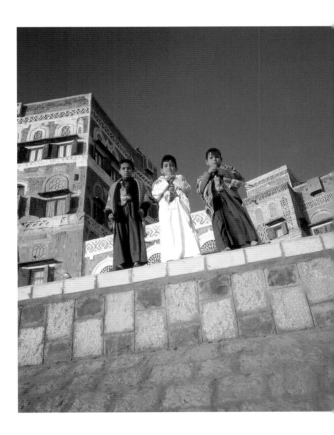

Chapter 1 - Dawn

6 am

THE RISING SUN FLARES ACROSS THE
rooftops of Al Hudaydah. All across
Yemen the sunlight of a new day
illuminates the markets and the early
morning traders. The fish market at Al
Hudaydah has been active for some
hours already, with the first of the
days catch already on sale in the
capital, Sana'a.

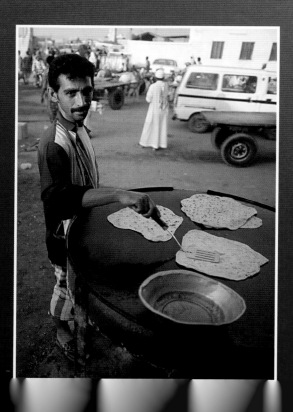

6.15 am

SOCOTRA BROKEN MONSOON CLOUDS CAST shadows over the Gulf of Aden between Socotra and Mukallah. Socotra is a unique island 500km south west of Al Mukallah. The vegetation of Socotra is a blend of species from the tropical African Sudan with the extra tropical Saharo/Arabian regions. 10% of the plant life is endemic, that is they occur nowhere else on our planet.

6.30 am

A BURST OF SUNLIGHT PENETRATES A
tower house complex in the Hadramawt
city of Shibam. On the other side of the
country, a farmer crosses the eastern plain
with his camel and cow. Elsewhere in
Shibam a shopkeeper prepares his
antiques for sale at the start of a new day.

Shibam is the most spectacular skyscraper city of Arabia. Tall mud buildings cluster so close together that they seem to be one structure, of almost uniform height - except for the Sultan's brown and white striped palace. With their plastered tops gleaming white in the morning sun, the buildings look most imposing. Their massive walls, sloping back slightly from their foundations, rise abruptly from the flat wadi bed. The majority of them are six or seven stories high, but appear to be twice that hight because each floor has a double row of windows, one above the other.

Inside the city, the buildings appear to be built on top of each other and only narrow alleys seperate them. Narrowness is not the only obstacle to a stroll down these alleys, for they are generally quite dark and full of people.

Shibam is the most important commercial town of the Hadhramaut. For centuries it has been the chief market for all surrounding tribes, and in recent decades has profited as the inland capital of the Sultan of Shilir

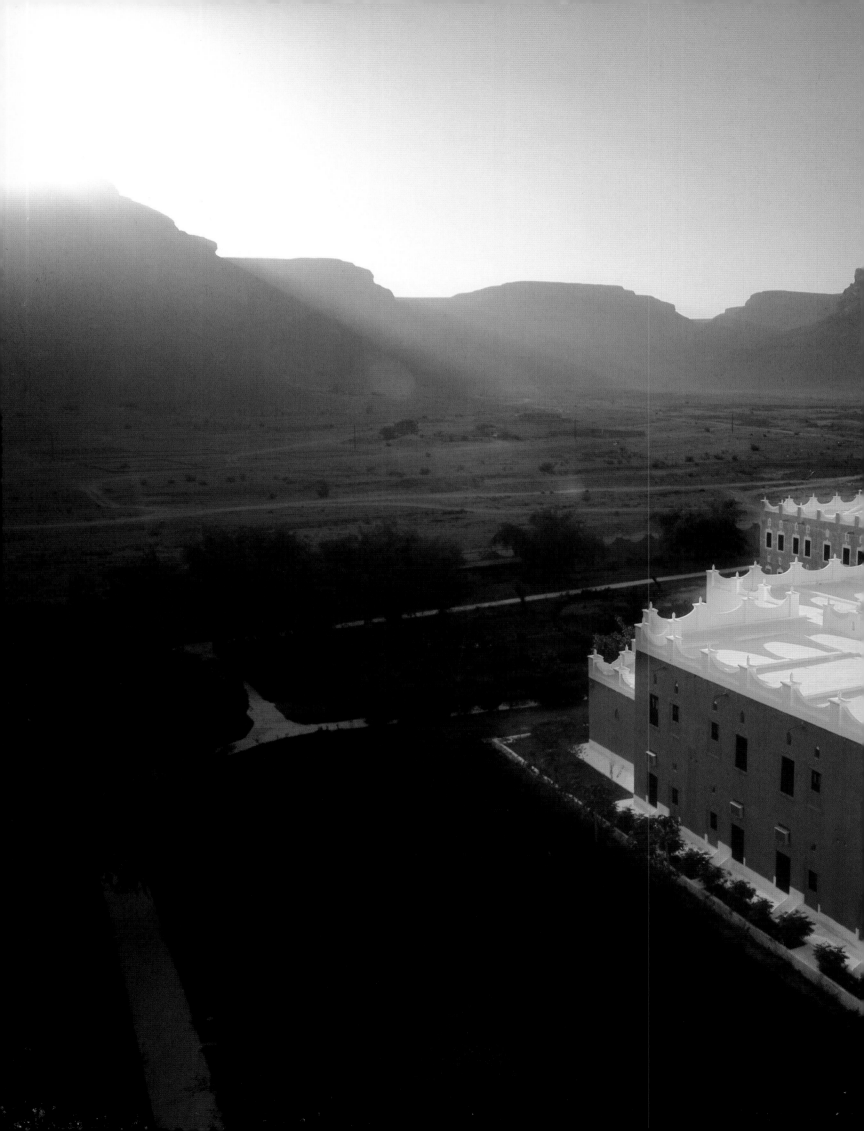

6.45 am

THE FIRST RAYS OF THE SUN ILLUMINATES the Sun Rise cafe while higher up the wadi the first kiln is lit. Two tons of wadi stones are placed inside the kiln which is then fired with a mixture of animal dung and oil, for the whole of one day. This firing process is called *Miffa*. The resulting white flaky powder called *Noorah*, is mixed with water to make a paste for water proofing mud-brick buildings.

7 am

BY 7AM, THE SUN HAS GIVEN COLOUR TO the high jebels and the first rays strike the very top of a renovated palace near Seyun. Nearby, intense heat is used in a kiln to break down wadi stones for use as a decorative white plaster.

7.15 am

BY 7.15 AM CHILDREN ARE WALKING TO
school along the sunlit canyons between
tower houses. Out in the fields modern
tractors are replacing traditional
donkey powered methods of farming.
The walled City of Shibam is known
throughout the world as the
"Manhattan of the Middle East". the
Tower houses are built entirely of mud
brick and taper towards their
uppermost floors. The windows are
carefully arranged having two windows
on each level to promote ventilation. In
turn, the windows give the impression
that the tower houses are twice as tall as
they actually are.

7.30 am

WHILE THE COCKEREL STILL STRUTS, school children gather in a mountain top school at Manakah. A shopkeeper has been selling flour for hours and the flour dust has already grizzled his beard.

7.45 am

THE PORT OF MUKALLAH HAS BEEN IN
existence for thousands of years. From
this port, Yemenis sailed in hand sewn
dhows, using primitive but effective
navigational methods devised by early
Arab sailors to reach destinations as
far afield as the East Indies and China.

8 am

IT IS SAID OF TARIM THAT WITHIN THE city there are as many mosques as there are days of the Islamic year - 354. The symbol of Tarim is the Al Mihdar Mosque; its unique architecture reflects the influence of South East Asia, which is still a popular destination for traders from the Hadramawt. Below, a proud young man walks from his tower house in Al Hajjaylah.

8.15 am

THE GREATER AND LESSER HUNAYSH
Islands lie some 50 kms due west of Al
Khukah on the Red Sea. Here, the
undisturbed coral reefs present fabulous
dive sites for visiting tourists. There are
five species of marine turtles in the waters
around Yemen; the green turtle, (Chelonia
mydas), the loggerhead turtle (Caretta
caretta), the leatherback turtle
(Dermochelys coriacea), the Oliver Ridley
(Lepidochelys olivacea) and the Hawksbill
turtle (Eretmochelys imbrictat).

8.30 am

SEYUN IS THE CAPITAL OF THE KATHIRI State of the Wadi Hadhramaut. The city centre is overlooked by the splendidly elevated Sultan's Palace which is built entirely of clay bricks. Within the palace is a museum and access to the roof provides expansive views across the city. Sayun has a long history dating back thousands of years which is covered impressively by three sections within the museum. These are; historical, folklore and a special section which displays the archaeological findings from the shrine of Mashad Ali. A team of Russian archiologists conducted an extensive dig, centred on Raybun, where a collection of clay mounds were excavated. The last Sultan of Seyun ruled until the late 1960's.

8.45 am

THE TOWN OF MARIB WAS FOUNDED IN 1200BC, in a strong defensive position overlooking the dam. The Roman General Aelius Gallus, was sent to gain control of the frankincense route but was defeated here at Marib. The city prospered from the levy of customs duties on the frankincense caravans and the vast supply of crops from well-watered areas around the old dam. The dam burst several times and was finally destroyed in 570 AD. The new dam, built at a cost of US $75 million, was a gift from Sheikh Zayed of the UAE to the people of Yemen. It was after the old dam burst that Sheikh Zayed's ancestors, the Bani Yas, migrated to the area now known as the UAE.

Chapter 2 - Morning

9 am

THE HIGHEST MOUNTAIN IN YEMEN IS Jebel Al Nabi Shu'ayb (the mountain of the Prophet Shu'ayb), at 3660m. The Jebel is situated 26km west of Sana'a and is the only mountain in Yemen which is occassionally, dusted with snow. On the slopes, beneath the peak, many crops are grown including coffee, sorghum, watermelons and grapes.

9.15 am

THE IMPRESSIVE NARROW ENTRANCE TO Kawkaban leads to a mountain top village with remarkable views over Shiban and on to Thula. While young men dance clutching their Jambuts, a more modern but modest young lady enjoyes her useful mountain bike. An elder from the village walks along the cliff top above a drop of several thousand feet and an impresive view of the village in the valley beyond.

9.30 am

LADIES WEARING TRADITIONAL STRAW HATS gather in the harvest. Extensive agriculture has made Yemen self sufficient but problems now loom as the ground water supplies become exhausted.

The Arabs of the Hadhramaut fared well in the great days of the incense trade, but when the rich kingdoms fell after transfer of the traffic to the sea, the wadi could not support its population. Hadhramis began to seek their livelihood in other lands, where they became tradesmen, real-estate owners, moneylenders and brokers. They settled in such distant places as Kenya, Tanganyika, Zanzibar, Sudan, Egypt, Saudi Arabia, Abyssinia, Singapore, Penang, and the former Netherlands East Indies, where the largest Hadhrami colony still flourishes. Wherever they went, however, they kept a deep love of their homeland. Despite the Hadhramaut's isolation, there has always been movement of people and goods between it and the Hadhrami colonies in other lands. This trade produced many modern luxuries including, jewels, imported foods and a college-educated upper class. As a result of the admixture of blood between Hadhrami Arabs and, in particular, the East Indians, Hadhramaut has been called the "Land of the Javanese Princesses".

9.45 am

THE CITY OF MAKALLAH, CAPTURED ON canvas by the renowned artist, David Shepherd. Apart from a modern road, the city has changed little. Against the mountain backdrop, the old port of Mukallah has been witness to centuries of sailing expeditions, setting forth to places such as India, the East Indies, Africa and China. Mukalla, a white city crowded onto a narrow shelf between the blue harbour and tall red-brown cliffs. Its white-washed buildings, of four or five stories, accented by the taller minarets of thirteen mosques, seem to rise up out of the water. Blue decorations on the houses pick up the colour of the sea, and four tiny white forts atop the cliffs complete the pictorial composition.

10 am

Dhow building continues today at Al Khukhah, where groves of palm trees separate the beach from the hot hinterland. The dhow craftsmen construct elegant vessels without reference to any plan, using only the simplest of tools including the plumb line. From a few ports hugging the narrow shore along the central portion of southern Arabia, trails fed into the main route to the north. Here strange vessels with huge sails swept in on the breast of the seasonal monsoons - whose variations were an oriental secret for thousands of years - to discharge cargoes from ports to the east, from India and from Socotra, the "Isle of the Blest", an important crossroad of sea trade between India, Africa and Arabia. Other harbours received goods from the nearby horn of Africa and sent them north to join the main road, which was worn deep by the flow of southern Arabia's priceless natural product - incense from the valley of the Hadhramaut and from Dhofar, the frankincense country.

10.15 am

SPRING CLEANING IN THE CLEAR WATERS of the harbour at Mukalla. As we watched the ambitious carpet washer, one of his carpets was washed into deeper water, it was rescued by a passing fisherman willing to jump overboard. Across the bay, guests from the Handramawt Hotel and the new Holiday Inn, scuba dive off the coral reefs and sport-fish in open seas. Sport fishing is the fastest growing sport of Yemen with relatively untouched waters. All varieties of sporting fish can be widely caught including sail fish, barracuda and tuna.

10.30 am

ZABID WAS FOUNDED IN 819 A.D. BY Moh'd bin Ziyad, whose dynasty ruled for more than 200 years. Zabid is the home of a university and here the architecture of the many mosques and Koran schools show a variety of influences from Egyptian to Turkish. Zabid is said to be the place where algebra was developed.

10.45 am

ON THE THIRD DAY OF A TRADITIONAL wedding, male guests celebrate by dancing, with flashing drawn daggers, to the mesmeric beat of the drum. Away from the crowd, a solitary figure stands on the cliff overlooking Wadi Dhar. The palace of Imam Yahya has now been converted into a museum.

11 am

A SPLENDIDLY ATTIRED YEMENI STANDS ON HIS rooftop while below, in the narrow streets, an itinerant barber finds a customer. Historical facts have been buried in the past twenty centuries though a few clues have survived the inevitable erosion of time. Legends and folk lore, many of which are romantic combinations of fact, fantasy and even poetry may contain some aspects of historical truth. The most reliable sources are the writings about southern Arabia by Herodotus, Pliny, Strabo, Eratosthenes and other classical writers, even though they are sketchy and often based on hearsay. The Periplus of the Erythrean Sea, one of the first factual accounts of the Yemen coastline by a Greek sea captain in the first century A.D., presented the first starting point for modern explorers. With the discovery of the sea route around Africa to India, early explorers, botanists and scientists were attracted by the clues to a fabulous past. These explorers braved the humid coast, the rugged mountains and the sandy wastes beyond. Everywhere, were feuding tribes whose only point of agreement was their hostility to foreigners, especially Westerners and Christians. During the past 150 years, a few men and fewer women have penetrated Yemen to describe the ruins of the great dam of Marib, which was one of the wonders of the ancient world. Adjacent to the dam, these early explorers found the wonderful Temples of the Moon.

11.15 am

THE FIVE MONOLITHIC PILLARS OF THE
Moon or Almaqah Temple stand on the
site also known as Arsh Bilqis - the
throne of Bilqis. The shafts of Jurassic
limestone, though partialy buried in the
sand, tower at least thirty feet into the
air. Near the top of the delicate stone
shaft is a beautifully carved circular sun
with a cresent moon while below is a
long Sabean inscription in perfectly
chiselled characters. Nearby is Bilqis
Temple (Mahram Bilqis) which was

excavated in 1952 by the famous Wendell Philip expedition. This temple is thought to date back to the eighth century BC. Two perfectly matched statues of a lion carrying a boy were found by the expedition near Timna. The workmanship in the two statues is very finely detailed. They were cast by a process called *cire perdue*. This method was known to the ancients and then lost for many centuries but is said to have been rediscovered by the great Italian sculptor of the sixteenth century, Benvenuto Cellini.

11.30 am

BEFORE UNIFICATION, AL HUDAYDAH WAS the
only habour in north Yemen which could
accommodate deep sea international
shipping. It is the second largest city in
Yemen and is the rival port to Aden. Today,
Hudaydah is the busiest of the three Yemeni
ports. Cargo vessels of all sizes depart from
this port to Djibouti, Aden, the east coast of
Africa and through the Sues Canal to the
Mediterranean and Europe. The permanently
anchored, brightly coloured tanker is a
transshipment vessel to other tankers who
call daily at this deep-sea port. The
hinterland behind Hudaydah is the Tihama
plain, literally meaning "Hot Earth", and
across this plain runs the main road
connecting the port to Sana'a.

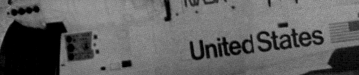

THE SPACE SHUTTLE COLOMBIA IS SHOWN orbiting the Earth at a height of 165 miles, 264 Kilometres at a speed of 25,000mph, 40,000Kph. The Colombia is flying along the approximate line of the Tropic of Cancer. The term was first used 2,100 years ago when the Greek astrologer, Hipparchus, calculated that the sun's highest point against the background of the stars, the summer solstice, was in the Cancer constellation. Since that time the axis of the Earth has changed due to the phenomenon of precission and now the Tropic should be called the Tropic of Gemini. High above Yemen, the astronauts study such phenomena. This remarkable photograph was taken by a free flying astronaut travelling in formation with the shuttle.

This is a view of the Red Sea with Yemen on the left and Eritrea on the right, leading down to the Bab Al Mandab "the Straits of Tears". Beyond the Straits and to the right is Djibouti while beyond is the Horn of Africa, Somalia.

Officially known as the Space Transportation System, the space shuttle has proved, despite one dramatic and disastrous mishap, a most efficient means of leaving the bounds of our planet Earth.

Along with the Apollo program which eventually landed on the moon, the shuttle is the major achievement of the US National Aeronautical and Space Administration (NASA) established after the soviets had gained a lead in space in the form of sputnik.

The first space shuttle was launched in 1981 and was called the Enterprise after the space craft in the TV adventure Star Trek. The first craft to prove the reusable theory was OV-102, the Colombia, shown here on a subsequent space flight.

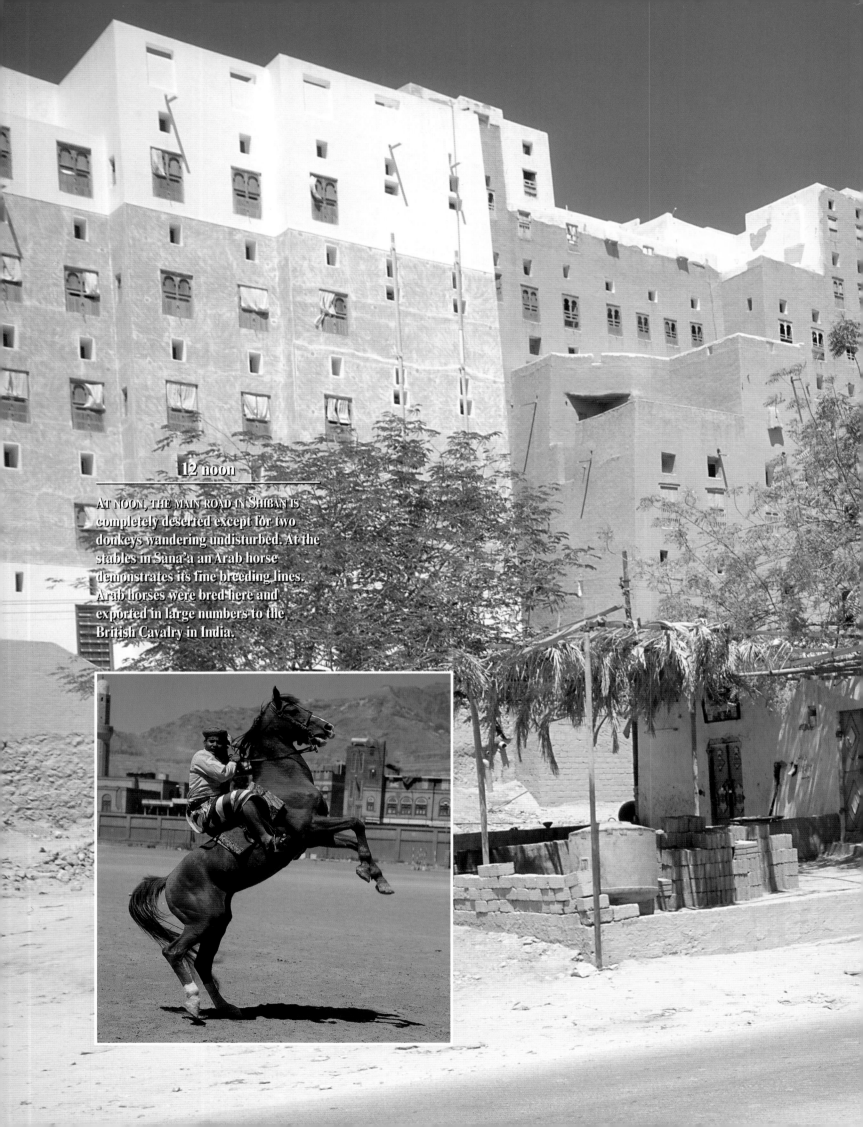

12 noon

AT NOON, THE MAIN ROAD IN SHIBAM IS completely deserted except for two donkeys wandering undisturbed. At the stables in Sana'a an Arab horse demonstrates its fine breeding lines. Arab horses were bred here and exported in large numbers to the British Cavalry in India.

Chapter 3 - Midday

12.15 pm

ON THE MOUNTAIN SLOPES, RAIN FALL
irrigates the terraced fields in a well
regulated manner. On the plains, the
continuous demand for water has
resulted in drilling down to depths of
2000 metres.

12.30 pm

LIKE FATHER, LIKE SON. AUTHOR AND son, Robert, walk from a Russian built helicopter operated by the Armed Forces of Yemen. A boulder roller works in the mountains while a tourist models the ubiquitous Khalashnikov rifle.

12.45 pm

THE MINEAN CITY OF YATHUL, NOW RECORDED ON THE MAP as Baraqish, is probably the best preserved, pre-Islamic ruin in the whole of Yemen. This fortress city is protected by a huge, 14-meter high wall incorporating fifty-two fortified tower houses. This city was on the frankincense route and the grandeur of the city was a reflection of the trade dues it collected from caravans passing from Marib en route via Najran, to Petra and on to Egypt and Rome.

The profits of trade were added to the profits of incense production, for southern Arabia was the great carrier of goods, the middleman between East and West. During the centuries when the Indian Ocean was a bustling center of maritime commerce - before the Mediterranean became the world's busiest shipping lane - the Arabs held a virtual monopoly of traffic between two civilizations that never came in direct contact with each other. Ships from India and Ceylon might stop at Arab ports on the Arabian Sea or barter in Arab-controlled regions of East Africa, where it curved in neighbourly proximity to the Arab homeland. However, they could not sail against the prevailing wind beyond the narrow strait of the Bab Al Mandeb, the entrance to the Red Sea. On the other hand, the ships of Egypt and other countries to the north could sail the relitively calm Red Sea, but their sailing skills were not sufficiently developed to go beyond the Bab al Mandeb into the Indian Ocean. Thus the middleman's position of the Yemenis was maintained by keeping producers and consumers apart.

Many of the Orient's luxuries, such as silks, porcelain and jewels were added to the loads of frankincense on the camel caravans from Southern Arabia, to the markets of the Western world. Various factions fought for control of the road as bitterly as they battled for the incense country itself. From the second millennium before Christ to early in the Christian era there was a succession of kingdoms that rose and fell, were conquered and disappeared. Such regional names as Saba, Main, Q'taban, Hadhramaut and Himyar, and their capitals, Marib, Qarnaw, Timna, Shabwa and Zafar. Of all these romantic names, the most familiar is that of Saba, also known by its other spelling - Sheba. The Queen of Sheba, mentioned in the Bible, visited King Solomon with many wonderful gifts, including frankincense.

1 pm

BY 1 PM, A NEW SESSION AT SCHOOL IS
about to start in Hudaydah while
inland, another school session has just
finished. With a population
approaching twenty million, the
government of Yemen is allocating
increasing resources for education
including the development of
Universities. In addition, many friendly
countries are contributing generously in
the form of scholarships to their
countries. Today Yemeni students can be
found in Germany, Holland, France,
the United Kingdom and the United
States of America. Returning educated
Yemenis now contribute to the running
of the country and have founded new
businesses ventures or have enhanced
existing companies.

1.15 pm

ADEN IS GEOGRAPHICALLY AND strategically located at the crossroads of the Red and Arabian seas with direct access to the Indian Ocean. The Port of Aden was, at one time, the world's primary ship bunkering port and the second largest bulk port. However, with the closing of the Suez Canal in 1967, Aden declined commercially. Now that the Canal is re-opened, the government of Yemen is re-building Aden into a world class, full service, international container terminal, transshipment hub and the largest industrial free zone in the world. This painting by David Shepherd of Slave Island shows the traditional Dhow building yards in the port of Aden.

- David Shepherd

1.30 pm

A YEMENIA AIRLINES A310 AIRBUS BRINGS tourists to Sana'a International Airport, within easy travelling distance of many of the spectacular mountain villages. Below, is the faculty of Medicine within the University of Sana'a.

1.45 pm

IN 1610, SIR HENRY MIDDLETON, director of the British East India Company, took to England the first sacks of coffee beans from the port of Al Makha. Thus developed the world wide trade in coffee and for about two centuries coffee was one of the most important products on the world market. Yemen had the trading monopoly in coffee, as it soon became one of the most popular drinks in the world. The Coffee plant (*coffee arabica*) is grown throughout the western mountains of Yemen.

2 pm

ELEPHANT BAY IS NAMED AFTER THE remarkable headland shaped like an elephants skull with a natural arch forming the elephants trunk. Ancient ancestors of the African and Indian elephants must have crossed the arabian land bridge during a previous ice age. At that time, vast amounts of water was frozen in the polar ice caps. The Red Sea and Indian Ocean were so low that the Bab Al Mandab (The Strait of Tears) was a completely dry land bridge. Other transients include Lions, Rhinoceros, Hippopotamus and our own ancestors, Homo sapiens. A distant relative of the Elephant, the Humpback Whale can still be seen breaching the water while Whale bones decorate a garage forecourt in Zinjubar on the coast of the Gulf of Aden. The Gold Mohur Sheraton Hotel in Aden, pictured right, is a haven for tourists and business travelers alike.

2.15 PM

THE ADEN OIL REFINERY WAS FIRST BUILT
in 1952 and was recently modernised.
The current production is 120,000
barrels of fuel per day. While Air BP
refuels the air force helicopter the
author shows fellow helicopter pilots
his previous book 'A Day Above Oman'

2.30 pm

THE OLD YEMENIS WERE ABLE TO LAUNCH various campaigns against the occupying Turks from mountain fortresses such as these. Here, the entrance to the fort is an open staircase above a pure vertical drop of 2000 metres. The Turks withdrew in 1636 AD but returned in the 19th Century.

2.45 pm

THE ADEN FREE ZONE HAS THE CAPACITY to handle up to 500,000 TEU's per year. Container s ships approach with confidence knowing that the approach channel is dredged to a depth of 16 meters and the harbour is one of the best protected in the world. In the 1960s, at the height of its prosperity, the port of Aden handled 600 ships every month. With the new facilities, Aden is poised to regain its former prosperity.

SHEIKH OTHMAN

MANSURA

AL-SHAAB

ADEN INTERNATIONAL AIRPORT

KHORMAKSAR

BANDAR AT TAWAHI

CALTEX

TAWAHI

MA'ALLA

CRATER

LITTLE ADEN

GULF OF ADEN

3 pm

By 3 pm. the shadows have already begun to lengthen into the valleys. On the parapet of a tower house, a solitary figure looks out on the descending, verdant terraces with a view towards Al Hajjayiah more than 50 Kms away. The distant mountain range where Al Hajjayiah is located rises up to 2,300 metres. Like the tower house shown, Al Hajjayiah is the major fortified settlement which dates back more than 800 years. The abundance of water in this region is collected by the inhabitants in natural stone cisterns which would enable any defenders to withstand a siege

3.15 pm

AL MUKALLA IS THOUGHT TO BE THE
departure point of the three Magi who
carried the gifts of gold, frankincense
and myrrh. Frankincense symbolizes
divinity and its value was equivalent to
gold. Today, in the old souq of Al
Mukalla, one can buy a handful of
frankincense for a few dollars.

3.30 pm

TWO YOUNG LADIES HOLD THEIR LAMBS IN
the mountain village of Al Hajjaylah. A
young man has a stall above the drop
into the valley looking towards Jebel Al
Urr, several kilometres away. A
popular item for sale is the silver Maria
Theresa dollars used in the past not
only as 'the' currency throughout the
Middle East but also as decoration.
The coins showing the Empress Maria
Theresa are all dated 1780, although

many have been minted recently. In the interior of South Arabia the Maria Theresa dollar, or riyal, was the only sizable coin accepted, despite the fact that Indian rupees and annas, were legal in Aden and official in the Qu'aiti and Kathiri states. Many still preferred the big and impressive M.T. dollar and did not really feel that they were getting money unless they saw the picture of the great empress of a nation of which they had never heard. The coin probably became current in Arabia by filtering down through the Ottoman Empire from Turkey long ago. Its value is approximately US $0.50, which fluctuates with the value of silver. The Bedouins of Beihan and Hadhramaut knew nothing of exchange rates, they only knew that they wanted the Maria Theresa dallars. However for small change, they accepted almost any small coins - local buqshas or money from India or the East Indies.

3.45 pm

THE TIHAMA PLAIN, BORDERING THE RED Sea, is a hot, dusty area. Tihama means "hot earth" and the inhabitants have adapted to the climate by building houses of straw that permit any cooling breeze to penetrate. The light, distinctive, hats offer perfect protection for those working in the fields growing millet and wheat.

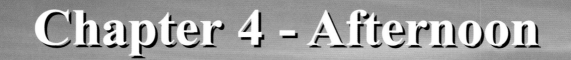

Chapter 4 - Afternoon

4 pm

IN VERY RECENT YEARS, WATER, electricity and graded tracks have reached the highest villages. For some, however, the traditional method of transport is still the most versatile, ever in the occasional mountain storms.

4.15 pm

THE WADI DOAN IS A MAJOR SIDE VALLEY OFF THE MAIN Hadhramaut wadi, where thick accumulations of silt are framed on either side by impressive Jebels. Irrigated fields of barley, interspersed with date gardens. The Wadi Hadhramaut is really a dried-up valley which occasionally floods. Many wadis are not dry all the time, but become raging torrents after heavy rains, when water pours down the cliffs and over the rocks unchecked by vegetation. For eleven months of the year, or often for several years on end, not a drop of water may be seen in many wadis, but sub-surface water may remain that can be reached by wells. There are many wells in the sixty-mile stretch of the Wadi Hadhramaut, near its source, accounting for the cluster of towns and villages in this area. At some points here the wadi is close to sixty Km wide, but gradually narrows to just a few Km beyond Tarim where the Hadhramaut becomes the Wadi Maseila. In earlier times, twenty thousand years ago, the Wadi Hadhramaut was a great river flowing eastward, fed by countless tributaries that are now the smaller wadis leading into the Hadhramaut. Genesis also refers to the sons of Joktan, and today one finds tribesmen of the Hadhramaut proudly stating that they are the descendants of Joktan. Legend tells us that Joktan is the great-great-great-grandson of Shem, son of Noah, and the legendary ancestor of all South Arabians.

4.30 pm

FRAMED IN THE HELICOPTER DOORWAY, THE
photographer captures a view that
reveals how men and women have
changed this landscape forever. Tower
houses, long lines of palm trees and
extensive cultivation form pleasing
patterns in a dramatic landscape. Here in
eastern Yemen, the tower houses are built
using mud bricks, a tradition that has
been followed for thousands of years.
The inner arrangement of the tower
follows a long established standard. The
ground floor is a stable for animals, the
floor above is used for storage and the
next floor up accommodates the servants.
Above this is the main family room or
diwan where guests would be received.

4.45 pm

EARLY EXPLORERS, SUCH AS RIMBAND IN
1885, Father Charmettan in 1878 and
Marshal Lyantey in 1894, all
complained that "there was not a
single blade of grass" in Aden.
However, when they penetrated to the
western highlands, they found
terraced cultivations that they termed
"a garden of paradise".

THE OLD TOWN OF MARIB DEPENDED ON BOTH THE DAM FOR AGRICULTURE AND frankincense for the customs duties it encouraged. Frankincense came from a scrub tree called *Boswellia sacra*. 2000 years ago, more than 3000 tons of this resin passed through Marib every year to the Mediterranean cities. Many legends have grown up around the Queen of Sheba, who was first mentioned in the tenth chapter of Kings chapter 1, which relates her famous visit to King Solomon in Jerusalem. At this time Solomon, who reigned from 961 to 922 B.C., had extensive shipping operations on the Red Sea and the Indian Ocean. As narrated in Kings, the Queen of Sheba came north by camel caravan. Her visit was of major commercial importance, for she "gave the King a hundred and twenty talents of gold, and of spices a very great store,

and precious stones; there came no more such abundance of spices as these which the Queen of Sheba gave to King Solomon".
Camels became domesticated about 3000 years ago when the need arose to transport vast quantities of goods across the deserts of Arabia. The journey

of the Queen of Sheba took place not long after the domestication of the camel and lead to the greatest expansion of trade in ancient history. In Isaiah, we learn that "The multitude of camels shall cover thee, the dromedaries of Midian and Ephah; all they from Sheba shall come; they shall bring gold and incense and they shall show forth the praises of the Lord". The Queen of Sheba may have been the ruler of the Sabeans while they were still a nomadic tribe because the first chapter of Job refers to the Sabeans as a raiding tribe; "And the Sabeans fell upon them, and took them away; yea, they have slain the servants with the edge of the sword; and I only am escaped alone to tell thee." The earliest rulers of this area were mukarribs who were the priestly rulers in the South Arabian kingdoms. Arab legends identify the Queen of Sheba with the name of Bilqis and there is mounting evidence of the fabulous fables that have grown up about her.

5.15 pm

THE RESCUE OF ARNOLD, ONE OF THE
last surviving Arabian leopards (*Panthera
pardus nimr*), was a wonderful example of
a three nation partnership. Arnold was
rescued from the souq in Sana'a,
transported in an aircraft sponsored by
an oil company and flown to the breeding
centre in Sharjah in the United Arab
Emirates. There Arnold mated and is
now the father of three Arabian leopard
cubs.

The last cheetah was killed in Wadi Mitan
in Yemen in 1963. Two more cheetahs

were killed at Ha'il in Saudi Arabia in
1973 and a cheetah was killed at Jibjat in
the Dhofar region of Oman in 1977.

There was also a confirmation that a
cheetah was killed in 1994 in Yemen and
Dr. Mohammad Al Mashjan of the
Environment Protection Council in
Sana'a confirmed that it was a cheetah
that had been shot. Moreover, the
remoteness of the area where it was killed
makes it unlikely that this was an animal
that had escaped from a private collection
and hence it is possible that cheetahs
might still exist. The cheetah,(*Acinonyx
jubatus*) in Latin, is called fehed hindi in
Arabic. It is the fastest moving four-
legged predator on earth. While charging
for a kill, it can reach speeds of more
than a hundred kilometers per hour, but
can maintain this speed for only a few
hundred metres.

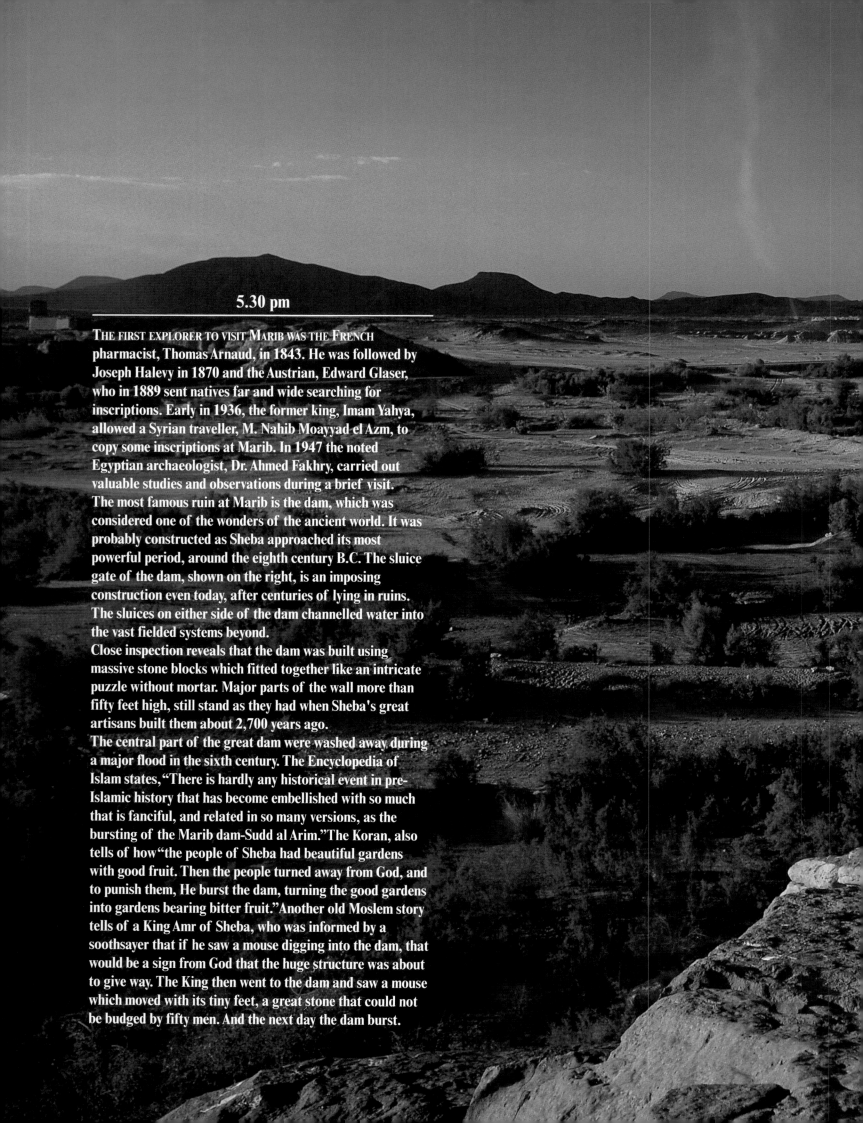

5.30 pm

THE FIRST EXPLORER TO VISIT MARIB WAS THE FRENCH pharmacist, Thomas Arnaud, in 1843. He was followed by Joseph Halevy in 1870 and the Austrian, Edward Glaser, who in 1889 sent natives far and wide searching for inscriptions. Early in 1936, the former king, Imam Yahya, allowed a Syrian traveller, M. Nahib Moayyad el Azm, to copy some inscriptions at Marib. In 1947 the noted Egyptian archaeologist, Dr. Ahmed Fakhry, carried out valuable studies and observations during a brief visit. The most famous ruin at Marib is the dam, which was considered one of the wonders of the ancient world. It was probably constructed as Sheba approached its most powerful period, around the eighth century B.C. The sluice gate of the dam, shown on the right, is an imposing construction even today, after centuries of lying in ruins. The sluices on either side of the dam channelled water into the vast fielded systems beyond.

Close inspection reveals that the dam was built using massive stone blocks which fitted together like an intricate puzzle without mortar. Major parts of the wall more than fifty feet high, still stand as they had when Sheba's great artisans built them about 2,700 years ago.

The central part of the great dam were washed away during a major flood in the sixth century. The Encyclopedia of Islam states, "There is hardly any historical event in pre-Islamic history that has become embellished with so much that is fanciful, and related in so many versions, as the bursting of the Marib dam-Sudd al Arim." The Koran, also tells of how "the people of Sheba had beautiful gardens with good fruit. Then the people turned away from God, and to punish them, He burst the dam, turning the good gardens into gardens bearing bitter fruit." Another old Moslem story tells of a King Amr of Sheba, who was informed by a soothsayer that if he saw a mouse digging into the dam, that would be a sign from God that the huge structure was about to give way. The King then went to the dam and saw a mouse which moved with its tiny feet, a great stone that could not be budged by fifty men. And the next day the dam burst.

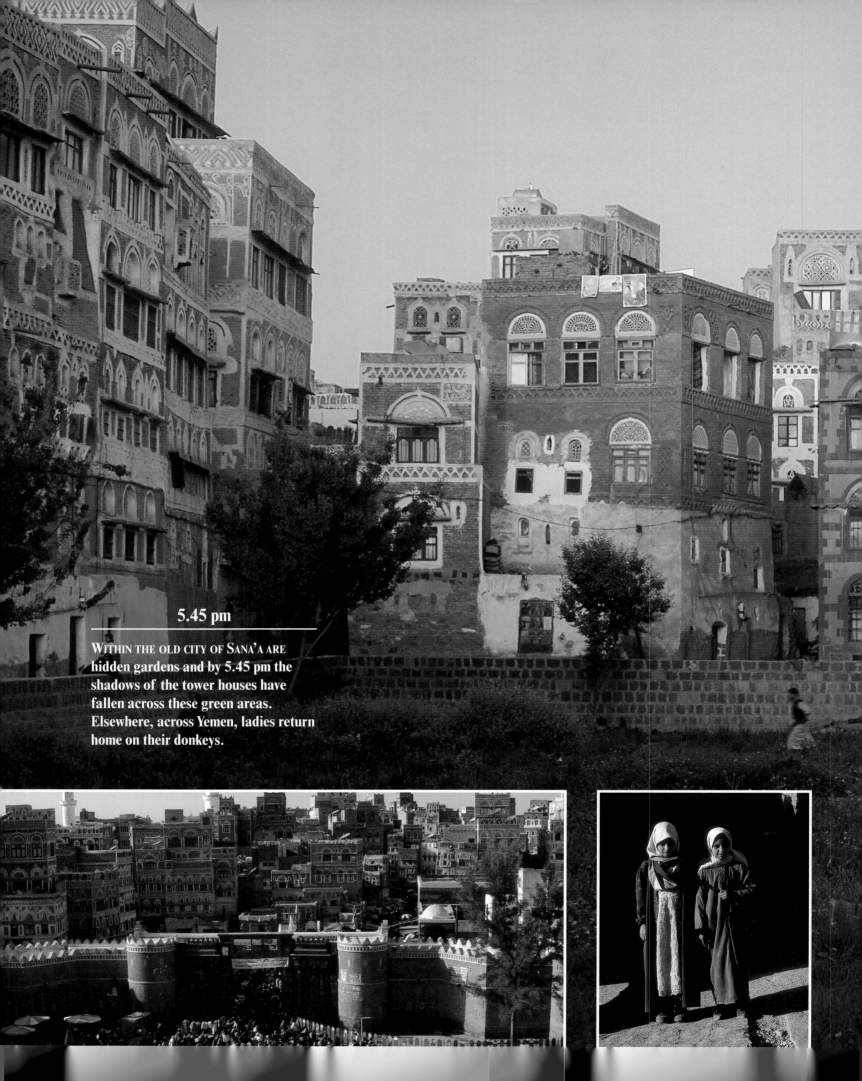

5.45 pm

WITHIN THE OLD CITY OF SANA'A ARE hidden gardens and by 5.45 pm the shadows of the tower houses have fallen across these green areas. Elsewhere, across Yemen, ladies return home on their donkeys.

6 pm

BY EARLY EVENING, A NUMBER OF football matches are in progress. The distant shouts echoed around the streets as the sun continued its slow descent to the horizon. On a roof top in Thula, a man entertains his guests to 'chai', arabic tea. In the Sana'a souq a vast array of glittering Khunjars are on sale.

Chapter 5 - Evening

6.15 pm

WARM SUNLIGHT BATHES THE ROOFTOPS OF SANA'A WHERE THE architecture has been unchanged for centuries. Sana'a stands on a high plain, some 2600 metres above sea level, surrounded by mountains. The old name of Sana'a is Azal, named after a descendant of Shem, the son of Noah.

6.30 pm

UNLIKE OTHER FORTRESS CITIES, SANA'A could depend on its privileged position as a place of *hijra*, a place of asylum and a city where all travellers could rely on safe passage. Today, Yemenis and travellers pass through the Bab al Yemen, the Gate of Yemen, continuing to build the prosperity of this beautiful city.

6.45 pm

THE DESCENDING SUN SILHOUETTES THE
jagged skyline around the Bab ash-
Sha'ub. Below in the gloom, the wadi
bed of the Sha'ila, a seasonal river is
confined by new improvements funded
by UNESCO.

Chapter 6
Author's
Acknowledgments

7 pm

In the first century BC, a Greek sailor named Hippalus, discovered that in the Indian Ocean the monsoon winds blow east toward India in the summer and west toward Africa in the winter. Soon Roman ships were able to bypass southern Arabia. Sea borne trade goods were transported from East to West at far less cost than overland by camel by avoiding the tax-levying cities.

Southern Arabia has been bypassed ever since, as the centre of civilization moved ever further away to the west and north. despite the passage of time, dolphins leap in the appropriately named Red Sea while near the airport at Aden, a flamingo stands alone.

7.15 pm

In the twilight of the setting sun four young Yemeni children walk along a restored wall which channels the occasional flood water through the old city of Sana'a. The walls were restored under a UNESCO project to preserve this world famous heritage site. Hundreds of miles to the East, a bedu lady enjoys the cool of the evening.

THIS PROJECT WAS BOTH THE LONGEST AND SHORTEST BOOK I have ever published. The longest because I first landed in Aden in 1966 having flown down the Red Sea and through the Bab Al Mandab, The Straight of Tears, at very low level. We then flew along the coast towards Mukallah and then inland to see the famed skyscrapers of the desert at Shibam before proceeding to Salalah in Oman and on to Singapore. From that first two-day glimpse, I knew I would be back but it wasn't until 1999 that the opportunity presented itself to initiate a publishing project. It later became the shortest project by going from conception to delivery in just three weeks including the aerial photography, design and layout, colour separations, printing and dispatch. Nick Crawley, my son Robert and I landed in Sana'a and 28 days later, the first 100 books were delivered to President Salah in Calgary by DHL very special delivery in time for his state visit.

I received a great deal of help from many officials, in
particular: His Excellency Ali Abdullah Saleh, President of
The Republic of Yemen for his support of the project, His
Excellency Abd Al Karim Al-Iryani, Prime Minister, Republic
of Yemen for his generous time, His Excellency Abdul Malik
Mansour, Minister of Culture & Tourism, who kindly wrote
the foreword, Moh'd Saleh Al Ahmar, the Chief of the Air
Force of Yemen and his many pilots and engineers who flew
us all over the country, Brigadier General Ali Hassan Al-
Shater and Mr. Abdu Boragi.

My family continue to give me great support, especially over
the Eid break, when the book had to come together; my wife
Christine, converted my RAF staccato text into English
English; Marc provided long distance internet support from
San Francisco; Kerri is still gaining 99% percentiles in her
medical studies at Sam Houston University in Texas; Robert,
now an accomplished photographer, backed me up in a
professional and artistic manner; Simone handled the proof
reading and yet more re-writing; Nicholas handled the
developing and mounting of the 2,600 pictures we took and
William, just 11 years old, handled all the internet
traffic, with attachments, between Dubai, Sana'a,
Washington and Calgary. My extended family of co-
workers, Juliette, Musarrat, Shibaz and Francis, missed
all the action due to the Eid Break but they sorted the
bombshell of our office when they returned. Four young
ambassadors of Yemen; Raasha, Hisham, Adam and Ryan,
deserve special mention, and Moh'd Lamjed El Kefi for his
underwater photography, pages 34-35.

In this, my third venture into self-publishing, I am grateful for
the professional help from my graphic designer/photographer,
Nick Crawley. In addition, we continue to enjoy world-wide
support from Images International in London, Premium

7.30 pm

Below, inset: The lights of tower houses start to come on.
Left: On the road leading east out of the city of Makulla, in
the direction of the Wadi Hadhramaut is this fort, the Hosn
wal Ghuazi. This fort, rising dramatically above the main
road, the symbol of old southern Yemen is already in deep
shadow. This fort, Makulla's major land mark, is built on top
of an amazingly shaped lava cliff and is the city's old
customs and guard house.

in Germany, Mon Tresor in Japan, Horizon in The Channel Islands, National Geographic in Washington and The David Shepherd Conservation Foundation. Large prints on art paper of his paintings; "Slave Island" and "Makallah", shown on pages 46-47 & 74-75, are available from Zodiac Publishing.

My thanks to the following companies whose support and encouragement made the publication of this book possible; Tim Thomas and Mr. Ali Sohaiki of Canadian Oxy; Abdul Khaliq Al Qasaily of MAPS, Yemen; Abdulkados Al-Beshari, MD of H & B; Captain Abdul Kalek Al Kadi, Chairman of Yemenia and Mr. Abdulwahab Sadaka, the Commercial Manager; Shaher and Hayel Abdulhak and Mayank Mehta of the Taj Sheba Hotel; Marco Livadiotti and his many driver-guides of Universal Travel for their support; the Aden Free Zone Establishment and finally Jeremy Bowen, Tim Bingham and Rick Capoccia of BP who have not only supported all my books but their very generous support helped to cover the costs of separations and printing.

The final round of thanks goes to six people who made this project an unforgettable experience; Faris Sanabani, Editor in Chief, The Yemen Observer; Moh'd Hiadra, my joint

MIDDLE EAST PHOTO LIBRARY

7.45 pm

The last rays of the setting sun light the ruins of the great dam of Marib. The remains of the dam above the pools are all that remain of this once great civilisation which was the richest in the world. Marib was founded in 1200 BC. and the fading light is a fitting tribute to this wonderful land and marks the end of another day – "Above Yemen".

and my son Robert. All share a valuable trait - the ability to laugh at overwhelming adversity and then to work or drive all night in taxis, to fix the problems and still do a very competent job the next day. These are the kind of people I like to have around and be around; who can be described as people who "when the going gets tough, the tough get going". With their help, this project, that was considered by many as mission impossible, was successfully and most memorably concluded. I think the effort was worth it.

John J. Nowell *LRPS FRGS*
Sana'a 2000

venture partner in Yemen; Hala Nasreddine, my colleague from The Washington Times; Antar Al Himyari from the Survey Department; Nick Crawley, my graphic designer/photographer

The
David Shepherd
Conservation Foundation

ZODIAC PUBLISHING

Al Jenaibi PHOTOGRAPHIC SERVICES

ZODIAC PUBLISHING

M E P L MIDDLE EAST PHOTO LIBRARY

P.O.Box 35121, Dubai, United Arab Emirates. Tel: 971 4 2826966 Fax: 971 4 2826882
e-mail: jjnowell@emirates.net.ae website: www.soorah.com GPS: N 25°14.912' E 055° 20.641'

TA.

Batoch.

Caras.

M. Oreb.

S. Cata-

rime.

Vagara

M.

P.T.

M. Anna

M. Lion

Anna

Loronj

Cozara

Cayhr

Bet.

Fara

Sinai m.

M. But.

AYAMAN

olim.

Farara

Adari

Eltor

Geuben.

Gabel. m.

ANNA

Chifale

Bubu:

Ianbog.

Porta di ferro arenofa

tor.

Genamani

Agaba

EGIAS.

ARABIA

de

Sicabo Ahelan

Elforga

ELCATI

Soridan

Medina Tal:

nabi vbi ma:

humetis

sepulchrum

vifitur.

Eltaif.

Lac

Gaibar

P. de Coßir.

Cana

Monte

Marzoan

Coßir

Zorma

Sati

Badrahenen

Rabech

Sabel m.

Ebeinedilig

Zimas. m.

Serta

Angotina

Farfi

Muy

Balamare

Zibith.

Rahon

Alinonuschi

P. Cotor

Mogal

Mecca

Sabalmay

Elferin

Vodora

Maru

bat.

Buga

Muchi

Ziden

Eda

Antax

Siler

Carscha

MARE DE MECCA, ET BOHARI. ET BOHARNVS

Slachi

Muchi

Carna

THEA:

Iasan.

Sagdech

Bul.

DAFILA.

Bul.

FE

Cibelrian

Ariadan

P. Maza Hali

braiti

Salta

Halibir

Cofonda

Iasuff

MA.

Nalober

Elferga

Babaua

Suachem

Suaché

Turuch

Barboni

Mugora

Siangar

Nifardroi

IRMI

Hirt

Zeiban

Adiudi

Lazama

Vi:

fart.

Hodieda

Menfura

COR SVN

Magot

olim

Zer

Zer

Cor.

Maha

Darsemas

Cana

Santar

Decor

ZIBIT.

Lacari

ARABICVS

Cubit

farif.

Elgent

Taesa

Dante

Mazuan

Zibith

Eldrin

luach

Ercoco

Camaran

Zilith

Zanaqu

Delacca, hic

margaritaru

piscatio.

Tuicce

Damear

ADEM,

REG

Mecca

Cacana

Pascoa.

Ara-

brewa Aden

Primera.

Vella

Docono

Babelmandel

Fretum

Belul.

C. Califin

Saladin

Hic Presbiter Io:
hannes totius Æe:
thyopiæ rex longe
latèq; imperitat.

Zeila

**Probably the best example of an artistic, highly
decorative map is Turcici Imperii Descriptio dated
1598 by Ortelius. Ortelius was considered one of the
greatest and most artistic map-makers of the 16th century because he put together, in 1570, the first uniformly
sized book of maps in Antwerp. The cartouches reflect the
baroque style of the time. The overwhelming detail, descrip-
tions and swash lettering make Ortelius easily identifiable.
"Swash lettering" is a term used to define the flourishing lettering sometimes used to fill in unwanted space on a map or to dis-
guise lack of knowledge of the area. Again, the importance given at
the time to the Ormus area, comprising mostly Oman and Iran, is shown
by the description of Ormus given to the right of the map. It indicates the
extent of Ormus, from the Euphrates to Cape Razalgate (the Portuguese name
for Ras Al Hadd) and that Ormus Island, known formerly as Gerun's Island,
was an important location containing an imposing fort - the gateway to the Gulf.**